DAVID

Man After
God's Own Heart

ROBBIE CASTLEMAN

FISHERMAN
BIBLE STUDY SERIES

DAVID

PUBLISHED BY WATERBROOK PRESS

12265 Oracle Boulevard, Suite 200

Colorado Springs, CO 80921

ISBN 978-0-87788-164-3

Published in the United States by WaterBrook Multnomah, an imprint of the Crown Publishing Group, a division of Random House Inc., New York.

Printed in the United States of America

2011

30 29 28 27 26 25 24 23 22

Contents

How to Use This Studyguide

Fisherman studyguides are based on the inductive approach to Bible study. Inductive study is discovery study; we discover what the Bible says as we ask questions about its content and search for answers. This is quite different from the process in which a teacher *tells* a group *about* the Bible—what it means and what to do about it. In inductive study, God speaks directly to each of us through his Word.

A group functions best when a leader keeps the discussion on target, but the leader is neither the teacher nor the "answer person." A leader's responsibility is to *ask*—not *tell*. The answers come from the text itself as group members examine, discuss, and think together about the passage.

There are four kinds of questions in each study. The first is an *approach question*. Asked and answered before the Bible passage is read, this question breaks the ice and helps you start thinking about the topic of the Bible study. It begins to reveal where thoughts and feelings need to be transformed by Scripture.

Some of the earlier questions in each study are *observation questions*—who, what, where, when, and how—designed to help you learn some basic facts about the passage of Scripture.

Once you know what the Bible says, you need to ask, *What does it mean?* These *interpretation questions* help you discover the writer's basic message.

Next come *application questions*, which ask, *What does it mean to me?* They challenge you to live out the Scripture's life-transforming message.

Fisherman studyguides provide spaces between questions for jotting down responses as well as any related questions you would like to raise in the group. Each group member should have a copy of the studyguide and may take a turn in leading the group.

A group should use any accurate, modern translation of the Bible such as the *New International Version,* the *New American Standard Bible,* the *New Living Translation,* the *New Revised Standard Version,* the *New Jerusalem Bible,* or the *Good News Bible.* (Other translations or paraphrases of the Bible may be referred to when additional help is needed.) Bible commentaries should not be brought to a Bible study because they tend to dampen discussion and keep people from thinking for themselves.

Suggestions for Group Leaders

1. Thoroughly read and study the Bible passage before the meeting. Get a firm grasp on its themes and begin applying its teachings for yourself. Pray that the Holy Spirit will "guide you into all truth" (John 16:13) so that your leadership will guide others.

2. If any of the studyguide's questions seem ambiguous or unnatural to you, rephrase them, feeling free to add others that seem necessary to bring out the meaning of a verse.

3. Begin (and end) the study promptly. Start by asking someone to pray that every participant will both understand the passage and be open to its transforming power. Remember, the Holy Spirit is the teacher, not you!

4. Ask for volunteers to read the passages aloud.

5. As you ask the studyguide's questions in sequence, encourage everyone to participate in the discussion. If some are silent, try gently suggesting, "Let's have an answer from someone who hasn't spoken up yet."

6. If a question comes up that you can't answer, don't be afraid to admit that you're baffled. Assign the topic as a research project for someone to report on next week, or say, "I'll do some studying and let you know what I find out."

7. Keep the discussion moving, but be sure it stays focused. Though a certain number of tangents are inevitable, you'll want to quickly bring the discussion back to the topic at hand. Also, learn to pace the discussion so that you finish the lesson in the time allotted.

8. Don't be afraid of silences; some questions take time to answer, and some people need time to gather courage to speak. If silence persists, rephrase your question, but resist the temptation to answer it yourself.

9. If someone comes up with an answer that is clearly illogical or unbiblical, ask for further clarification: "What verse suggests that to you?"

10. Discourage overuse of cross references. Learn all you can from the passage at hand, while selectively incorporating a few important references suggested in the studyguide.

11. Some questions are marked with a ✎. This indicates that further information is available in the Leader's Notes at the back of the guide.

12. For more information on getting a new Bible study group started and keeping it functioning effectively, read *You Can Start a Bible Study Group* by Gladys M. Hunt and *Pilgrims in Progress: Growing Through Groups* by Jim and Carol Plueddemann. (Both books are available from WaterBrook Press.)

SUGGESTIONS FOR GROUP MEMBERS

1. Learn and apply the following ground rules for effective Bible study. (If new members join the group later, review these guidelines with the whole group.)

2. Remember that your goal is to learn all you can *from the Bible passage being studied.* Let it speak for itself without using Bible commentaries or other Bible passages. There is more than enough in each assigned passage to keep your group productively occupied for one session. Sticking to the passage saves the group from insecurity ("I don't have the right reference books—or the time to read anything else.") and confusion ("Where did *that* come from? I thought we were studying _____.").

3. Avoid the temptation to bring up those fascinating tangents that don't really grow out of the passage you are discussing. If the topic is of common interest, you can bring it up later in informal conversation after the study. Meanwhile, help one another stick to the subject.

4. Encourage one another to participate. People remember best what they discover and verbalize for

themselves. Some people are naturally shy, while others may be afraid of making a mistake. If your discussion is free and friendly and you show real interest in what other group members think and feel, the quieter ones will be more likely to speak up. Remember, the more people involved in a discussion, the richer it will be.

5. Guard yourself from answering too many questions or talking too much. Give others a chance to share their ideas. If you are one who participates easily, discipline yourself by counting to ten before you open your mouth.

6. Make personal, honest applications and commit yourself to letting God's Word change you.

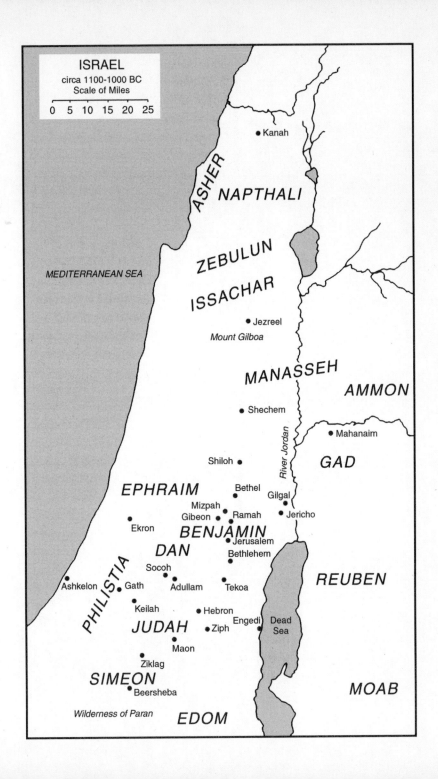

Introduction

I began a study of David during a "dry spell" in my Christian life. The demands of mothering two boys, both under two years of age, left little time for "quiet time" with God. One day, between diapers and dishes, I was reading Acts and this verse "leaped out" from the page:

> After removing Saul, he made David their king. He testified concerning him: "I have found David son of Jesse a man after my own heart; he will do everything I want him to do." (Acts 13:22)

Oh, that's what I wanted too! I wanted to be a person after God's own heart, God's "kindred spirit," obedient and blessed. I wanted to know God as David must have known him. I longed to be the person God honored with such a testimony.

I wondered how David lived such a life and how I could be like him. I didn't have any "Goliaths" to slay or lions to kill; nor was I in a position to move a whole nation to worship. As I pondered what I knew about David, I realized that my knowledge consisted mainly of a few famous stories. I had never studied David as a whole person—his character and spiritual growth.

So I began to study the life of David. Every morning before my household awoke, I delved into the personal history of a man who, in spite of his sin, his inconsistencies, his life full of pressures, knew God and loved him.

David's story is set at the beginning of a new millennium—about 1000 BC. It seems like a very long time ago, in a remote, barbaric, and unenlightened era. But I was surprised to discover how little people and their problems have changed in three thousand years.

Israel, after coming out of Egypt under Moses' leadership and conquering the Promised Land in a rather patchwork way, remained a very loosely organized, tribal nation for three hundred years. Ruled by God's law alone, the nation's only leaders were the local judges.

Before long, however, the tribes, yearning to be strong and self-sufficient like the nations that surrounded them, chose to go the way of monarchy. Their first king was fine by all appearances, but his life took tragic turns, leading the people with him. The second king—to be known as the greatest of all Israel's kings—was David. His rise to the throne was full of intrigue, politics, and difficult lessons. His reign united the nation.

Through this study, I saw a David who knew the delights and difficulties of belonging to God and being loyal to him in spite of the world's pressures. I saw him stumble in his walk with God and suffer the consequences. But I also saw David, the king, bowed in obedient submission to the Lord of his life. And I also discovered that I have "Goliaths" to battle and my own little "kingdoms" to lead joyously to the Father's throne. God touched my heart again with his love for me through David's son, my Savior.

STUDY 1

HOW CAN I CHOOSE
GOD'S BEST?

1 SAMUEL 16

B ut why not?" If you've been around children much, you've heard this question countless times. From their limited perspective it is hard to understand why they can't have what they want. As adults we often relate to God in the same way. The Israelites demanded, "Why can't we have a king like the other nations?" (see 1 Samuel 8:19-20). So God gave them Saul as their first king. Saul's life was a story of self-reliance and disobedience, and God finally rejected him. This time God would give the Israelites *his* choice for king, and they would learn that God gives the best.

1. Can you think of a situation when you've seen that God's choice for you was better than what you wanted at the time? *God gave me Dave my husband instead of childrens Fathers.*

READ 1 SAMUEL 16:1-13.

Difference with the Two

2. Contrast the appointment of Saul with the appointment of David (1 Samuel 8:19-22; 16:1). List the differences.

3. Why was Samuel hesitant to anoint a new king (verse 2)? How did the people react to Samuel's arrival? Why? *Cause Saul will Kill him They trembled, Cause he has come to sacrifice unto the Lord,*

4. *First Born* Who was Eliab? What first impressed Samuel about him? *Jesse's Son, cause of the Lord is annoited and his Sacrifice, Leader of the Division of the tribe of Zebulun, Leading worship in the temple, also brough animals to sacifrice as a Fellowship offering.*

5. How clearly did God indicate his choice? What is important to God (verse 7)? *Look on his countenance The Lord seeth not as man seeth, man Looketh on the outward appearences, but the Lord Looketh on the heart.*

he DID obey God

6. How careful was Samuel to obey God? Do you keep listening to God even after you have what seems like a good idea? *They DID not obey and Take the Lord's Advice. I go what the Holy Spirit tells me, (I try).*

7. David was only a teenager at the time of his anointing. What help did God give him? What difficulties do you think he might have encountered as he continued to live in his father's house? *The spirit of the Lord after he was annointed*

READ 1 SAMUEL 16:14-23.

8. The Spirit of the Lord came upon David and departed from Saul. What took its place in Saul's life? How did Saul's servants deal with this problem?
evil spirit which God allowed it pride Destroyed him.

Indicates further information in Leader's Notes

9. Describe David's qualifications for the job (verse 18). How would each of these characteristics be important for David's success as a king?

Cunning in playing   comely person
mighty Valiant man
man of war
prudent in speech

10. What was the basis for the initial relationship between David and Saul? What was there for David to learn in this situation? *he loved him greatly and became his armourbearer.*

Favor in his sight

11. As you wait for God's purposes to be fulfilled in your life, how can you continue to learn?

with the Holy Spirit

We should modeled by God

12. In summary, what have you seen in David that shows he was a person "after God's own heart"? How can you begin to develop some of David's characteristics in your own life?

David Chose to follow God with all his heart, he put God First before anything else, he made a point to Keep his heart Pure & Devoted To God

HOW DO I FIGHT GOD'S ENEMIES?

1 SAMUEL 17

There is something very satisfying about someone winning out against overwhelming odds. Whether it is a small country defending itself against a bully dictator or a completely unknown runner taking a world-class race, we instinctively admire the tenacity and courage it takes and cheer them on.

This familiar story of David and Goliath has become a common metaphor for underdogs defeating giants. In this classic confrontation, David meets his first serious test as God's anointed successor to Saul. Visualize the scene: the opposing armies amassed for battle, a bellowing warrior with a very large ego, and a young man with five small stones and much faith. God's glory is at stake, and David is ready.

1. How do you respond when someone ridicules your faith? *My spirit Just quenches and I cant get back into it till I pray about it.*

READ 1 SAMUEL 17.

2. Who are the main players in this chapter? Describe the battle setting. *Phillistines armies Israelite armies*

David Goliath

In my bible under 17:1

3. Paint a word picture of Goliath (verses 4-11). How did Saul and the Israelites respond to the giant's challenge? *a champion who was 6 cubits, helmet of brass upon his head, armed with a coat of Mail, greaves of brass upon his legs, brass between his shoulders*

9 feet Tall

Afraid

4. How long did the impasse continue before David's arrival (verse 16)? What effect do you think the continuation of the unanswered challenge would have had on the army of Israel? *40 days*

5. Why was David sent to the battlefield (verses 17-18, 20)? *Jesse comanded him*

6. What incentives were the men of Israel given to kill Goliath (verse 25)? What was David's incentive (verse 26)? *will enrich him with great riches give him his daughter, make his Fathers house free in Israel*

uncirmcised Philistine that he should defy the armies OF The Living GoD

7. How does big brother Eliab react to David's questions? Why? *his anger was kindled Left those few sheep in the wilderness pride + naughtiness of Thine heart for thou art come down that thou mightest See the battle.*

8. What reason does David give Saul for his confidence (verses 34-37)? *Verse 37 he will deliver me out of the hand oF this Philistine.*

9. In spite of his blessing in verse 37, what else did Saul see as essential for winning a battle? Where did *his* confidence lie? *the LorD was with him, with the LorD*

10. Summarize the action of verses 41-51, and visualize yourself in David's place. Describe the various emotions he must have felt at different stages of the encounter with Goliath.

11. How important are size or other physical qualifications in God's economy? What can God do with "unqualified" people who have faith and obey him?

12. What have you learned from David about reasons for success or failure? Do people know there is a God in your life? How?

2 Timothy 1:7
Acts 9:31

Do not be afraid
fear not

HOW SHOULD I
HANDLE MY FEARS?

1 SAMUEL 18:1-16; 19:1-18; 20

Max Lucado says, "I don't mind being a pilgrim as long as I can call home as often as I want to." In times of uncertainty and distress, it's reassuring to have a "home base." As David rose to fame in Israel, he became the object of King Saul's irrational hatred and soon was fleeing for his life. But in the midst of this chaos, God provided a home base for David—friends and protection—teaching David that he could turn to God in a crisis.

1. How do you usually respond to a crisis? Why?

READ 1 SAMUEL 18:1-16.

2 What new relationship enters David's life (verses
1-4)? How might this make things easier for him?
How might it also complicate his life?

Jonathan
They both made a convenant
because he Loved him as his own
soul.

3. Who is pleased with David's new prominence, and
why (verses 5, 7, 16)?

Sauls servants
David's 10 thousands
All of Israel and Judah

Cause, He went out and came
in before them.

4. What negative emotions begin to grow in Saul
(verses 8-15)? *evil spirit*
Very wisely

Very wroth and displeased
Jelously, Affraid

5. What repeated phrase (verses 12, 14) gives the secret
of David's growing success? What character qualities
does David display in this chapter that show he is
following after God?

And the Lord was with him

he had Love beyond Degree
he was humble, obedient, wise

READ 1 SAMUEL 19:1-18.

6. How does Jonathan speak with his father about Saul's reasons for taking David's life (verse 5)? How effective was his plea (verse 6)?

will thou sin against innocent Blood.

Saul swared, as the Lord Livith he shall not be slain.

7. What reason did David have to fear for his life (verse 10)? Describe how David escaped from Saul. Where did he go?

Saul smote the Javelin into the wall.

He slipped away out of Sauls presence

Psalm 59

he fled and escaped that night

Note: Michal may have resorted to idol worship (note the "household idol," verse 13) because she was barren.

Michal Let David down through a window and he went & fled

READ 1 SAMUEL 20.

8. Why does David come to Jonathan (verse 1)? What does this show you about David?

Cause he knew he sinned

He is Like you and me that when you know you sinned we would come to GoD.

9. Describe the covenant love between Jonathan and David (verses 8, 13-17, 23, 41-42). How lasting and deep was it? Friends for a Lifetime Lasting Convenant

It was touching, they with each other + kissed each other

10. Why was Jonathan concerned about making this covenant with David?

11. What impresses you most about the relationships in these tense and emotional scenes?

READ PSALM 59.

12. David wrote this psalm after his escape from Saul. What does David affirm about God? Could you "sing praise" in similar circumstances?

DO I TRUST GOD WHEN I'M UNDER PRESSURE?

1 SAMUEL 21–22

Years ago there was a popular television series called *The Fugitive*. Week after week the falsely accused victim would narrowly escape the police hunting him. No matter where he turned, he could never really trust anyone or reveal his true identity. In this next chapter of David's life, he too lives as an innocent fugitive relentlessly pursued by Saul. David is driven to extreme measures to stay alive, and in the process he makes some decisions that he later regrets. David learns the hard way that it is better to depend on God than on his own strength.

1. Can you think of a time when you have taken a situation into your own hands? What were the consequences?

READ 1 SAMUEL 21:1-9.

2. After being convinced of Saul's intention to kill him,
   where does David go? In what practical ways does
   Ahimelech help David? *To NOb To*

   AhimeLech the priest

   He was affraiD oF meeting DaviD

3. What could have been David's motives for lying to
   Ahimelech? On whom was David relying for his
   safety? *Taking matters in his own hanDs*
   DaviD is relying on God, he is
   Fearful

READ 1 SAMUEL 21:10—22:50.

4. Gath was a Philistine city. Find it on the map (p. xi).
   How did David handle being recognized here?
   What insight do you gain about David's character
   from this incident?

   he was affraiD -Verse 13

   mad man

5. Locate Adullam on your map, in north central
   Judah. Who joins David at Adullam (22:1)? Why
   do you think his whole family moved to Moab?

   about 10 miles SE oF Gath I 16 miles sw
   oF Jerusalem. His brethen + all his Fathers
   house.
   Verse 2 chapter 22

6. Why did the 400 men join David at Adullam? What characteristics of David would have been most important in dealing with such a motley group?

David was down and discouraged so God brought people around him to strength him. He was annointed by God to be next King.

7. Who commanded David to leave the stronghold and return to Judah (22:5)? Why would this have been a dangerous move? What was God teaching David about real security? *Prophet Gad*

prepare him for the Kingdom, and uphold and increase his reputation among the people God wanted David to Learn to trust

READ 1 SAMUEL 22:6-23.

8. How was the rivalry between Saul and David escalating? What indications of Saul's instability can you find in this passage (verses 6, 8, 13, 17)?

9. What characteristics did Ahimelech display when questioned by Saul about helping David (verses 14-15)? How did Ahimelech assess David's real attitude toward Saul? *so Faithful, honorable he was still Loyal*

10. What tragic consequences had resulted from David's "simple" lie in 1 Samuel 21:2ff.? Put yourself in David's place—how would you have felt as you made the statement of 22:22?

11. What principles of trust can you learn from this story of David? *Putting your all Faith and trust in the Lord.*

12. When you're afraid, how do your actions and decisions reflect or fail to reflect your trust in God?
I Just put my Faith in the Lord and keep trusting him.

DOES GOD REALLY DELIVER?

PSALM 34

This psalm sheds light on what was stirring in David's heart and mind while he was fleeing from Saul. He had lied and pretended to be insane to ensure his own safety and escape from enemies. He wrote this psalm afterwards, revealing a repentant and trusting heart. David originally wrote this psalm—like much other Hebrew poetry—as an acrostic, in which each verse begins with a successive letter of the Hebrew alphabet.

1. Review the narrative of 1 Samuel 21:10–22:2. Pretend you are David. What emotions do you feel during these events?

READ PSALM 34:1-7.

2. How did David view God? How did he view himself? How can insignificant humans magnify the God of the universe?

He was always praising God.
He changed his behaviors

3. List all the verbs in these verses, identifying which refer to David's actions and which refer to God's.

bless,   *exalt*   *Lightened*
Shall continually   *Sought*   *cried*
hear   *heard*   *saved*
glad   *delivered encamped*
magnify   *Looked*   *delivereth*

4. Describe a time when you have experienced God's deliverance from fear or trouble. Does the assurance of verse 7 change your feeling about God? About circumstance? How?

READ PSALM 34:8-14.

5. How can we "taste" and "see" the Lord today? Translate these metaphors into the language of your own experience. *IF you Keep Trusting and believing in him.*

Trust
Fear

6. Rephrase the promise of verse 10 and the condition on which it is given. What would this have meant to David in hiding? *The Lord is a Sun and a Shield: he will give grace + glory, no good thing he withhold from them that walk uprishtly,*

7. In verses 13-14 is the fear of the Lord seen in inner attitudes or outward actions, or both? What is the "fear of the Lord"? *I would say both verse 13 is outward and verse 14 is inner.*

respond to him in obedience.

READ PSALM 34:15-22.

8. Identify the different kinds of people mentioned in these verses. How does the Lord relate to each of them? *righteous - Delivereth out of their Troubles Contrite Spirit - the Lord Saveth Wicked. he Desolates them*

9. Recall the types of people who joined David in Adullam (1 Samuel 22:2); how would verse 18 have applied to them? Share a time when you have felt "brokenhearted" or "crushed in spirit" yet have felt the Lord's comfort and closeness.

10. According to verse 19, what is the lot of the righteous? In what does their hope lie? How can "troubles" be part of the abundant life in Christ?

    The Lord will always Delivereth all.

11. Select and memorize a verse in this psalm that will help you to fear the Lord in the deepest and best sense. *Verse 14*

HOW DO I MAKE DECISIONS?

1 SAMUEL 23–24

Brutus pierced Julius Caesar. Judas kissed Jesus. Betrayal is a particularly disheartening and devastating act. As David and his men continue to evade Saul's army, they face betrayal and hardship as never before. It would make sense for David to take revenge on his betrayer and destroy his enemy when he gets the chance. In spite of the pressures of his circumstances and other people's opinions, David learns to make decisions based on God's will, no matter how crazy it may seem.

1. Have you ever been betrayed by someone? Share how you felt when it happened.

READ 1 SAMUEL 23:1-5.

As you read, locate each place-name on the studyguide map.

♪ 2. Why do you think David was told of the Philistine
siege against Keilah? What was David's dilemma in
this situation (verses 2-3)? Was the advice of David's
men practical?

They were affraid.

3. On what basis did David act against the advice of
his associates? What happened at Keilah?

READ 1 SAMUEL 23:6-18.

♪ 4. Why did Saul plan to attack David at Keilah? What
was David's first response when he heard of Saul's
plan?

5. In verses 10-12 the Lord confirmed that the men
of Keilah would deliver David and his men into
the superior power of Saul if they stayed in the city.
How might this have made David feel about his
earlier decision to defend Keilah?

6. David and his now six hundred men escaped to the rocky, cave-pitted wilderness of Ziph. If you had been David, why would the meeting with Jonathan have been particularly encouraging at this time? In what ways did Jonathan encourage David (verses 16-18)?

READ 1 SAMUEL 23:19-29.

7. How did Saul respond to the information he received from the Ziphites? Where were David and his men hiding?

8. How was David delivered from Saul? In the light of David's betrayal by the men of Keilah and the Aiphites, what do you think David would learn from his deliverance here?

READ 1 SAMUEL 24:1-15.

9. How did David's men assess the circumstance of Saul's entering their cave (verses 3-4)? What was David's response to this tempting opportunity?

10. Observe David's posture and hear the tone of his words in verses 8-15. How did he view his relationship with Saul? With God?

READ I SAMUEL 24:16-22.

11. Describe Saul's response to David. Where did Saul and David then go? Why might David have had reason to distrust Saul's response?

12. Do you let your circumstances (or the reactions of others) become "God's will" for you? Share specific instances in your life when you may have wrongly assumed God's will by the appearance of your situation or the opinions of other people.

13. Read Psalm 54. David wrote this when betrayed by the men of Ziph. How does this psalm reflect David's development into a man "after God's own heart"?

DO I LISTEN TO GODLY COUNSEL?

1 SAMUEL 25

It's been said that we find comfort among those who agree with us and growth among those who do not. Often, though, we resist the growth that disagreements and unwanted counsel offer. When David finds himself in a disagreeable situation, he receives some good advice, which saves him from the consequences of an impulsive decision. The outcome makes a fascinating love story!

1. When someone offers you advice, how do you usually take it?

READ I SAMUEL 25:1-17.

2. After Samuel's death, where did David go? What help did he and his men provide for Nabal in the wilderness (verse 16)?

3. A reward was customarily given for such service; what reasons are given for Nabal's negative attitude and reaction (verses 3, 10-11)?

4. What was David's reaction to Nabal's insults? What recent events in David's life may have contributed to his outburst of anger?

5. From the description given to Abigail by Nabal's servant, what do you learn about the character of David's band of fugitives (verses 14-17)?

Read 1 Samuel 25:18-35.

6. Make a list of adjectives that describe Nabal. Make a similar list of Abigail's characteristics. What attitudes and character qualities can you avoid or imitate?

7. Briefly summarize Abigail's intervention effort. Was her reason for meeting David limited to her desire to save her family?

8. Abigail had a prophetic understanding of the Lord's intentions for David. How did she remind David of God's promises and protection (verses 26, 28-31)?

9. Consider David's response to Abigail's appeal (verses 32-35). What character qualities are evident in David?

READ 1 SAMUEL 25:35-44.

10. Summarize briefly the resolution of the story in terms of the three main characters: Nabal, Abigail, and David. How might the story have ended if David had not listened to Abigail?

11. In what ways did God provide for David and Abigail?

12. Share instances of how someone's godly advice has caused you to change a hastily made bad decision.

AM I TENSE OR TRUSTING?

1 SAMUEL 26–27

A Persian proverb exhorts us to "trust in God, but tie your camel tight." We trust God, but what does it hurt to have a few safety nets under us too? This is how David operates as Saul continues to hunt him. In his mounting desperation, David begins acting out of fear and disobedience in an effort to protect himself.

1. What are some sources of anxiety or discouragement for you right now?

READ 1 SAMUEL 26.

2. Compare the main events of this chapter to the events of 1 Samuel 24 when David encountered Saul in the cave.

3. Who betrayed David for the second time (verse 1)? How large a military force did Saul use to pressure David? What other signs of anxiety were evident in Saul (verses 5, 21)?

4. What was David's response to Abishai in verse 9? In whose hands did Saul's fate rest (verse 10)?

5. Because of his growing anxiety, what decision did David anticipate with dread (verses 19-20)?

READ 1 SAMUEL 27:1-7.

6. With whom did David consult as he made his decision to leave Judah? How was he disobedient to the earlier command of the prophet Gad (see 1 Samuel 22:5)?

7. On his arrival in Gath for the second time, David was welcomed as an outlaw and a known enemy of Israel's king. What were the results of David's move (verses 4-7)?

READ 1 SAMUEL 27:8-12.

8. What did David do in Ziklag (verse 8)? What did he tell Achish he was doing (verse 10)?

9. Review the accumulation of tension and anxiety in David's life through 1 Samuel 25–27. Identify his various moods and their causes.

10. David took the easy way out and left Judah. What reasons did David have for continuing to trust God by staying in Judah?

What reasons do you have to go on trusting God in your life?

11. How does this study of David help you to know how to deal with tensions and fears? Be specific.

HOW DO I RELATE TO GOD AFTER FAILURE?

1 SAMUEL 28:1-2; 29–30

Part of maturing as a Christian involves owning up to and facing the consequences of your sin. Weary of Saul's pursuit, David had fled, and he now found himself in a real predicament because of his disobedience.

In spite of David's failure to trust God, God had not forsaken him and was leading him by circumstances toward a renewed trust relationship. Lessons in trust are often painful and sometimes have to be learned through the removal of all support and help but God himself. But God's help is always there, and David's renewed relationships with other people reflect the restoration of his relationship with God.

1. When you have really "blown it," do you turn to God or keep your distance? Why?

READ 1 SAMUEL 28:1-2; 29:1-11.

✐ 2. War eventually erupted between Philistia and Israel.
   What might have been David's internal reaction
   when informed that he must fight against Israel?
   (Observe the ambiguity of David's reply in 28:2.)

3. How did the Philistine commanders react when
   they learned of the presence of David and his men?
   What two reasons did they have to be suspicious of
   David (29:4-5)?

4. How did Achish describe his relationship with
   David (29:3, 6, 9)? In spite of this, what decision
   did he make regarding David?

5. In what way was David's reply ambiguous again?
   Was it likely that David would have ever really
   fought against Israel (see 1 Samuel 27:8-11)?

Read i Samuel 30:1-6.

6. Imagine the tragic scene as David and his men returned "home" to Ziklag. How was the intensity of their grief demonstrated?

7. Why would the resentment and rebellion of his troops drive David to the Lord? How do you think he "found strength in the LORD"?

Read i Samuel 30:7-19.

8. What was David's pressing concern at this point? What reassurance did he receive?

9. Briefly describe the rescue. What made the ambush of the Amalekites possible?

10. What happy discovery did David make (verses 18-19)? How does the phrase "nothing was missing" speak to you about the completeness of God's forgiveness and provision?

READ 1 SAMUEL 30:20-31.

11. What was the problem that developed over the division of the plunder? Contrast David's attitude with that of the "troublemakers" in verse 22.

12. How did David renew his contact with his own people (verses 26-31)? How is David now better prepared for the responsibility of kingship?

13. When you have been forgiven and blessed by God, what changes should you see in your actions and relationships with other people?

AM I WILLING TO "LOSE MY LIFE"?

1 SAMUEL 31–2 SAMUEL 1

We like to live under the illusion that we can control our lives. At times we seem to be doing such a good job of regulating things that God becomes irrelevant—at least until it all falls apart and we don't know why. Saul was a controller too. He was so busy grasping after power and trying to protect himself that he never stopped to listen to what God might have wanted for him. David had his times of managing his own life as well. Yet his heart remained teachable and open to God. In this study we learn of the sad results of one life lived independently of God and the maturing response of another life entrusted to God.

1. When someone you dislike gets his or her "just deserts," how do you feel?

Read i Samuel 31.

2. How thoroughly were the men of Israel defeated (verses 1, 7)? What significance did the death of Saul's three warrior sons have for David's future as king?

⊘ 3. What was Saul's overriding concern after he was wounded? What irony did the next day reveal (verses 8-10)?

4. How did his last words and actions reflect the pattern of his life as we have observed it?

5. Who intervened to end the disgrace of Saul and his sons? Why did they risk their lives to recover the bodies? (See 1 Samuel 11.)

6. There was no national mourning for Saul. What did this indicate about the state of the nation of Israel at that point?

Read 2 Samuel 1:1-16.

7. What inconsistencies are there between the two narratives of Saul's death that might indicate the Amalekite was lying (compare verses 6, 8-9 with 1 Samuel 31:4)? What might have been his motive for bringing Saul's crown and bracelet to David?

8. How did David and his men express their grief? Why do you think David had the Amalekite killed?

Read 2 Samuel 1:17-27.

9. How did David refer to Saul and Jonathan in his lament? Why was David so grief-stricken?

10. David's longtime "enemy" had fallen, and David mourned. What did David omit from his lament over Saul? Why?

11. Discuss how the completeness of God's forgiveness can affect your forgiveness of others.

12. Saul, who held his life so tightly, died by his own hand. David, who refused to grasp at the crown, became Israel's next and greatest king. Read Matthew 16:25 and discuss it in the light of the lives of Saul and David. Is there something in your life to which you cling tightly? How does this study encourage you to "let go" and trust God with your life?

CAN I TRUST GOD'S TIMING?

2 SAMUEL 2–3:1

Most things of real value take time: mastering an instrument, forging out a career, developing relationships. Life is a slow process of growth by failing and succeeding, waiting and going forward. This was true back in David's day too. Even with Saul dead, David learns that becoming king of Israel will take time. He reigns as a tribal king of Judah, but he must continue to hold his own against Saul's successors. God uses this long period of civil war and waiting to bring about an even stronger king and a united kingdom.

1. How do you respond when you have to wait in line for something?

READ 2 SAMUEL 2:1-7.

2. As the chapter opens, what was David's first action? Did he seek general or specific guidance? What was God's answer?

3. What took place in Hebron?

4. Why did David contact the men of Jabesh-Gilead? Why did he think it important to do this?

READ 2 SAMUEL 2:8-17.

5. How long was Ishbosheth king of Israel? Who exercised the real power during his reign, and how?

✑ 6. What did the hand-to-hand battle at the pool of Gibeon accomplish?

READ 2 SAMUEL 2:18–3:1.

7. How would you describe Asahel? What may have been his motives for pursuing Abner (verse 21)?

8. What reason did Abner give Joab for wanting to stop the fighting (verse 26)? What action did Joab take, and why?

✑ 9. What change is described in 3:1? What were the implications of this change for David politically, spiritually, and personally?

10. Why could David afford to be patient during these years in Hebron? On the other hand, why would waiting have been hard?

11. Think of the "in-between places" in your life. Why is it difficult to trust God during those times? What reasons do you have for trusting God anyway?

Close in prayer, thanking God, with David, that our times are in God's hand. Pray for clear insight in understanding what God wants to teach us in these waiting times.

HOW DO I TREAT
MY ENEMIES?

2 SAMUEL 3:2-39

Following the Civil War a member of Abraham Lincoln's cabinet voiced his desire to destroy their enemies in the South. Lincoln thoughtfully replied, "Do not I destroy my enemies when I make them my friends?" David follows this same strategy as he endeavors to bring reconciliation and unity to the fragmented kingdom of Israel. In a world of easy revenge, David chooses God's way of mercy toward his enemies.

1. Is there a "peacemaker" in your family? What effect does this have on your family relationships?

READ 2 SAMUEL 3:2-12.

✒ 2. Over what situation did Abner and Ishbosheth clash? What did this action indicate about Abner's view of himself and his role?

3. What does verse 9 tell us about Abner's appraisal of God's revealed intention for David?

4. From what you have learned about Abner, what was the real reason he defected to David?

5. Abner was guilty of "convenient obedience," submitting to God's will and word only when it served his own purposes. Relate a time when you have treated God and his will "conveniently." What happened?

Read 2 Samuel 3:13-21.

6. David's position as king over all of Israel was now being consolidated. Why was it politically expedient for David to have Michal again for his wife? (See 1 Samuel 18:27.)

7. How would you describe Israel's attitude toward David during Ishbosheth's reign? What did this mean for David?

8. Why did David make a feast for Abner? What did this reveal about David's attitude toward his enemies and his strategy for becoming king?

Read 2 Samuel 3:22-39.

9. How would you explain Joab's motives and actions? How did Joab's politics differ from those of David?

10. What reasons did David have for such a public and elaborate mourning for Abner?

11. From David's example, what can you learn about how to treat your enemies?

STUDY 12

HOW DO I HANDLE
SUCCESS?

2 SAMUEL 4–5

After years of struggle and anguish, David finally celebrates his kingship over all of Israel. God had worked mightily to bring him to this point, and there must have been a welcome sense of grateful relief among the people of Israel. Success can be difficult to handle, but David reveals his heart for God in the midst of his greatest victory.

1. Relate one of your most satisfying achievements.

READ 2 SAMUEL 4.

2. Considering what you know of Abner's role under Ishbosheth's reign (2 Samuel 2:8-9; 3:6), why do you think the king and all of Israel were afraid when Abner died?

3. What seemed to be the motives of Recab and Baanah for killing Ishbosheth? Why did they think Ishbosheth's death would please David?

4. What was David's reaction? To whom did David give credit for his success?

5. What reasons did David have for the execution and public display of the bodies of the two murderers? Consider both legal and political reasons.

READ 2 SAMUEL 5:1-16.

6. What three reasons did the tribes of Israel give for wanting David as their king (verses 1-2)?

⌀7.   What was the "first order of business" after David became king (verses 6-7)? Why was this helpful in establishing a unified Israel?

⌀8.   How does Scripture record the "secret" of David's greatness (verse 10)? How do you think David felt when the city of David was established?

9.   David's reflective realization of God's work in his life helped him to trust God more. Do you stop and take stock of God's dealings in your life from time to time? Why is it important for you to do this?

READ 2 SAMUEL 5:17-25.

10.   Why would this victory over the Philistines be particularly encouraging for David and the "new Israel"?

11. What did this show about David's ability to handle success?

12. How is David's reliance on God shown in these battles?

13. How is your reliance upon God reflected in your prayer life? How does dependence upon God help you handle success?

DO I DELIGHT TO DO GOD'S WILL?

PSALM 40

Have you ever had something wonderful happen that you couldn't wait to share with someone? That's the vibrant feeling with which David writes this psalm—wonder and gratefulness for what God has done for him. It is not known when in David's life this psalm was written, but it illustrates well his understanding of God.

1. Share a way in which you've seen God's faithfulness to you.

READ PSALM 40:1-8.

2. From what you have learned about David, identify specific times in his life when he "waited patiently" for God's help.

3. To what events might he have been referring in verse 2? What was David's response to God's deliverance (verse 3)? Share times when you have experienced this particular kind of intervention by God in your life.

4. What are two ways to demonstrate trust in the Lord, according to verse 4? How do the truths of verse 5 encourage trust?

5. God had rejected Saul from being king of Israel because, though he "sacrificed," he didn't "obey" (see 1 Samuel 15:22-23). In light of verses 6-8, what do we know David had learned? What was the source of his obedience (verse 8)?

READ PSALM 40:9-17.

6. List all the things "proclaimed" by David in verses 9-10. What seems to be his motive for speaking out?

7. How did David describe his sin (verse 12)? How did this confession help David seek God for deliverance?

8. What impact does the recognition of sin in your life have on you? How is your attitude reflected in the way you confess your sin?

9. List all the things David asks of God in verses 13-17. What do you remember about events in David's life that make verse 14 true of him?

10. How could David "wait patiently" (verse 1) and still express his needs so urgently, as in verse 17? Discuss situations in your life where you can learn to wait patiently as well as pray fervently.

11. Select a verse from this psalm that speaks clearly to you in your present circumstances. Write it out here, and memorize it.

12. Identify principles you have learned from the life of David for having a heart for God. Pray together, asking the Lord to make these concepts real and effective in your lives.

Leader's Notes

STUDY 1: HOW CAN I CHOOSE GOD'S BEST?

Question 8. You may wonder how an evil spirit could come from God. There are several possible explanations of this phrase. *Evil* here may be used in the sense of "troubling." The *Wycliffe Bible Commentary* suggests that "a gloomy, suspicious melancholy, bordering on madness, affected the mind of Saul. To the Hebrew, every visitation, of good and evil alike, was directly from God" (p. 286).

Question 12. The phrase "after God's own heart" refers to the fact that David became God's "kindred spirit," someone "to God's liking," one in whom God found a special affinity or delight.

STUDY 2: HOW DO I FIGHT GOD'S ENEMIES?

Question 2. Israel was fully equipped for battle and repeatedly shouted a war cry yet never came to grips with the enemy forces and conquered them.

Question 4. Some scholars believe that several years had passed since David had served in Saul's court. Others say that perhaps the events in 1 Samuel 16:22 *followed* those of 1 Samuel 17 (see 1 Samuel 18:10). Either way, 1 Samuel 17:55-58 could simply imply that Saul did not know much about David's family.

STUDY 3: HOW SHOULD I HANDLE MY FEARS?

Question 7. See map to locate Ramah in relation to Jerusalem. Samuel lived here, leading an active school of prophets, and was later buried there.

Question 10. Jonathan recognizes that David will be king one day. Though this could have been *his* right, Jonathan is not jealous or bitter. This covenantal pledge becomes more important to Jonathan than his loyalty to his father or his own desires to be king. Later, David keeps his promise by caring for Jonathan's son, Mephibosheth (2 Samuel 9).

STUDY 4: DO I TRUST GOD WHEN I'M UNDER PRESSURE?

Question 4. "Why did the Philistines accept their archenemy, David, into their camp? The Philistines may have been initially happy to accept a defector who was a high military leader. Any enemy of Saul would have been a friend of theirs.... Soon, however, the Philistines became nervous about David's presence" (*Life Application Bible,* Wheaton, IL: Tyndale House Publishers, p. 474).

Question 5. The book of Ruth tells the story of David's great-grandmother. Ruth was a Moabitess.

Question 8. Apparently Saul's retinue of servants was all from his own tribe of Benjamin (1 Samuel 22:7). This may have reflected Saul's growing paranoia about the allegiance of the people around him.

STUDY 5: HOW DO I MAKE DECISIONS?

Question 2. Keilah was a city whose economy was based on the growth and harvesting of grain. It was in Judah, south of Adullam.

Question 4. The ephod was a linen vest worn by the high priest. In addition to twelve gemstones representing the tribes of Israel, it held a loose pouch or small box containing two or three stones or discs, known as the Urim and Thummin. It is uncertain, but perhaps to determine God's will in "yes or no" situations, the stones or discs were flung out and their position interpreted. The Hebrews had absolute confidence in the sovereignty of God and his control over the casting of these "lots." (See Exodus 28:29-30; 1 Samuel 14:41.)

Question 7. Maon was a flat plain, leaving David in a vulnerable position, away from the protection of the mountains.

Question 9. Rising six hundred feet above the Dead Sea, En Gedi was a well-watered rocky bluff, pocketed with vast limestone caves. Saul pursued David there and entered a cave in order to re-lieve himself. He probably laid his robe aside, thus enabling David to cut off its edge unobserved (1 Samuel 24:4). In those times, a man's robe was a significant symbol of his person, almost like an extension of himself (see 1 Samuel 18:4). This may account for David's remorseful reaction after cutting the robe (1 Samuel 24:5).

Question 12. God may indeed use circumstances to direct our lives, but they must be viewed along with other guidance factors (such as prayer, biblical principles, and the advice of Christian counselors) and not as God's sole means of leading us.

STUDY 6: DO I LISTEN TO GODLY COUNSEL?

Question 2. Nabal means "fool" in Hebrew, denoting not mere stupidity but moral perversity. It suggests one who is insensitive to the claims of both God and man and who is consequently at once irreligious and churlish (*The Wycliffe Bible Commentary*, p. 290).

Question 4. David may have been disappointed and discouraged about the outcome of his obedience to God in sparing Saul's life. His godliness had not brought about immediate restoration. Samuel's death may well have added to his depression and impatience.

Question 8. The metaphor in 1 Samuel 25:29 reflects the common practice of binding valuable things in a bundle to prevent their being damaged.

STUDY 7: AM I TENSE OR TRUSTING?

Question 5. The Hebrew idea of deity at that time was still fairly territorial. For the Hebrews, the Lord was in Israel, and to leave the land may have signified to David that he would also leave the protection of Israel's God—a false assumption, as he would later realize.

Question 6. The full consequences of David's decision to leave Judah will be realized in the chapters ahead.

STUDY 8: HOW DO I RELATE TO GOD AFTER FAILURE?

Question 2. "David was in a quandary, but could only comply. There is dramatic irony in Achish of Gath designating David...as his bodyguard, for not many years later Gittites were to provide David's bodyguard" (*New Bible Commentary, Revised*, p. 301).

Question 7. "Faced with the tragedy of losing their families...[the soldiers] looked for someone to blame. But David found his strength in God and began looking for a solution instead of a scapegoat" (*Life Application Bible*, p. 486).

STUDY 9: AM I WILLING TO "LOSE MY LIFE"?

Question 3. The armor bearer was the king's bodyguard and was answerable for the king's life.

Question 7. "The stories are not irreconcilable.... It is possible that [Saul's] own sword-wound did not immediately have fatal effect. However, it may be best to view the Amalekite's tale as either exaggerated or partly untrue" (*New Bible Commentary, Revised*, p. 302).

STUDY 10: CAN I TRUST GOD'S TIMING?

Question 3. David was thirty years old and would rule in Hebron for seven and a half years as king of Judah.

Question 5. There is historical speculation that Ishbosheth was physically and/or mentally handicapped. Though he was forty years old when he became king, there are no records of his involvement in battles or of his having a wife or children. He appears to have been a puppet king for ambitious Abner, reigning only for the last two of David's seven-and-a-half year reign. It had taken five and a half years to regain land lost to the Philistines, and only then could a government be reestablished.

Question 6. The contest of 2 Samuel 2:12-17 was a means of limiting bloodshed by involving only one or more representatives from each side, rather than two armies. David's heroic contest with Goliath was another example.

Question 9. The "long war" that took place between Judah and Israel was a cold war. There was little or no armed conflict between them.

STUDY 11: HOW DO I TREAT MY ENEMIES?

Question 2. Concubines were thought of as the exclusive possession of the throne's heir, and to approach one was like claiming the throne. A "dog's head" means a traitor.

Question 6. Since Michal was Saul's daughter, it's likely David thought having his wife back would strengthen his claim to rule over Israel.

STUDY 12: HOW DO I HANDLE SUCCESS?

Question 7. Up to this time, Jerusalem had been an impenetrable city, and the Jebusites were mistakenly self-assured in their security. They felt that even their "lame and blind" citizens could repel David's forces. (David sarcastically mocked them as being all "lame and blind" after his conquest was complete!) Before David's conquest of Jerusalem, there had been no central gathering place for Israel. There had been several temporary places where Israel could congregate (Shiloh, Mizpah, Nob, Hebron) but no capital city. David recognized the need for a centralized government, and by making Jerusalem the permanent capital, he helped establish national unity.

Question 8. 2 Samuel 5:13-16 continues the listing of 2 Samuel 3:2-5. All of David's sons born in Jerusalem are listed here even though all certainly had not yet been born.

The Fisherman Bible Studyguide Series—
Get Hooked on Studying God's Word

Old Testament Studies

Genesis

Proverbs

New Testament Studies

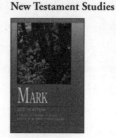

Mark

John

Acts 1-12

Acts 13-28

Romans

Philippians

Colossians

James

1, 2, 3 John

Revelation

Women of the Word

*Becoming Women
of Purpose*

*Wisdom for
Today's Woman*

Women Like Us

*Women Who
Believed God*

For more information, visit our Web site: www.waterbrookmultnomah.com

Topical Studies

Building Your
House on the Lord

Discipleship

Encouraging
Others

The Fruit of the
Spirit

Growing Through
Life's Challenges

Guidance and
God's Will

Higher Ground

Lifestyle Priorities

The Parables of
Jesus

Parenting with
Purpose and Grace

Prayer

Proverbs &
Parables

The Sermon on
the Mount

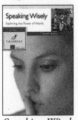

Speaking Wisely

Spiritual
Disciplines

Spiritual Gifts

Spiritual Warfare

The Ten
Commandments

When Faith Is
All You Have

Who Is the
Holy Spirit?